ALFRED's
ACRED PERFORMER
COLLECTIONS

MW00562125

10 Christian Worship Favorites

Arranged by **Kenon D. Renfrow**

In my experience, the popularity of worship music is due, in large part, to the theological depth of its texts. Other factors that contribute to its appeal are pleasing melodies that are easy to sing and are highly memorable, as well as the manner in which the texts and melodies are wed.

Because of the important truths conveyed through this music, I encourage you to look up the texts to these songs and reflect on them as you communicate through your performance. I find that even practice sessions can become worship experiences when reflecting on the texts. May you receive blessings from playing these worship favorites, as you reflect on the great truths found within.

Kenon D. Renfrow

ALFRED

Produced by
Alfred Music Publishing Co., Inc.
P.O. Box 10003
Van Nuys, CA 91410-0003
alfred.com

Printed in USA.

ISBN-10: 0-7390-8390-2
ISBN-13: 978-0-7390-8390-1

(Approx. Performance Time – 3:45)

MERCIES ANEW

Words and Music by
Mark Altrogge and Bob Kauflin
Arr. Kenon D. Renfrow

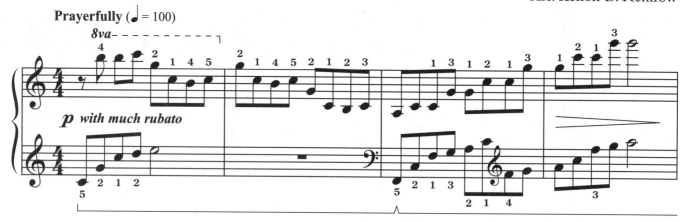

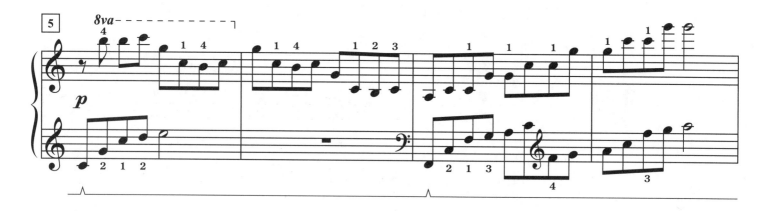

(Approx. Performance Time – 5:00)

THE LOOK

Words and Music by
Bob Kauflin and John Newton
Arr. Kenon D. Renfrow

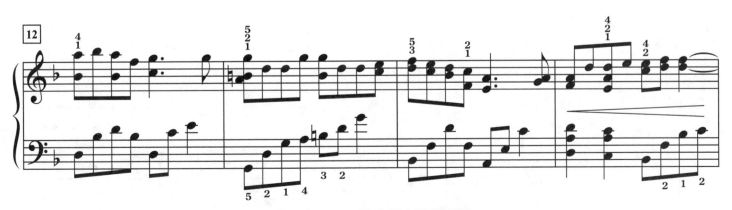

BEHOLD THE LAMB
(COMMUNION HYMN)

Words and Music by
Keith Getty, Kristyn Lennox Getty and Stuart Townend
Arr. Kenon D. Renfrow

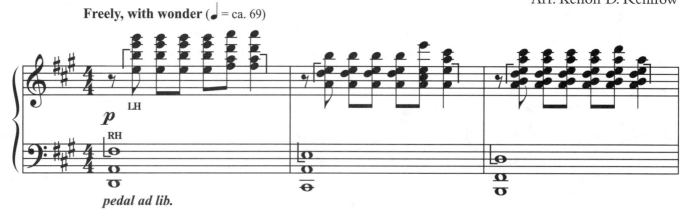

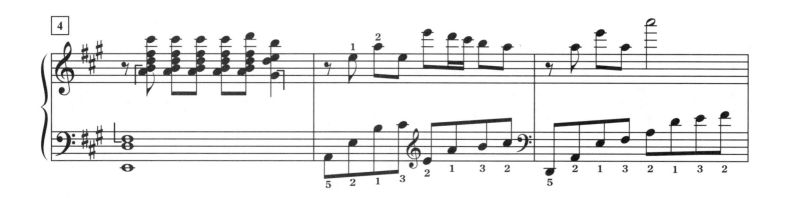

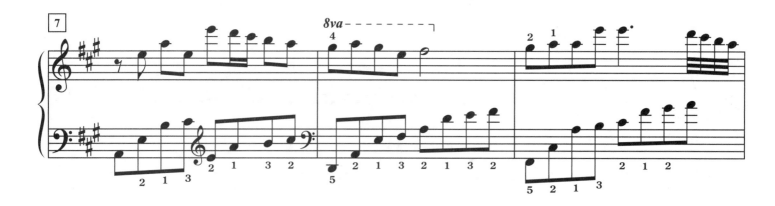

(Approx. Performance Time – 3:00)

Knowing You
(All I Once Held Dear)

Words and Music by Graham Kendrick
Arr. Kenon D. Renfrow

(Approx. Performance Time – 4:00)

THE WONDER OF THE CROSS

Words and Music by Vicki Beeching
Arr. Kenon D. Renfrow

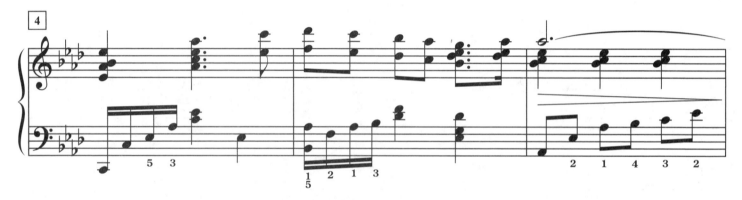

Broader

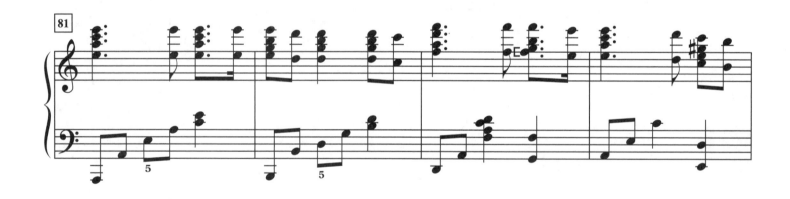

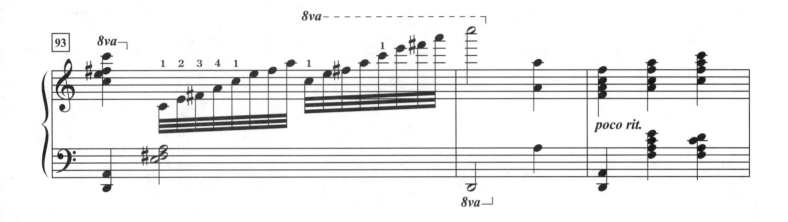

You Are My All in All

Words and Music by Dennis L. Jernigan
Arr. Kenon D. Renfrow

28

(Approx. Performance Time – 4:00)

DRAW ME CLOSE

Words and Music by Kelly Carpenter
Arr. Kenon D. Renfrow

(roll when necessary)

(Approx. Performance Time – 4:15)

ABOVE ALL

Words and Music by
Paul Baloche and Lenny LeBlanc
Arr. Kenon D. Renfrow

Gratefully (♩ = 72)

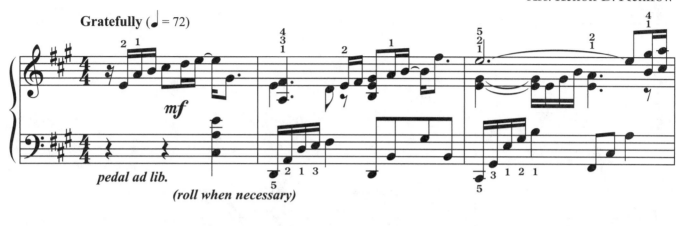

TRUST HIS HEART

Words and Music by
Eddie Carswell and Babbie Mason
Arr. Kenon D. Renfrow

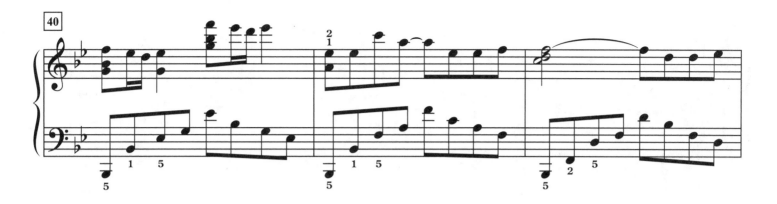

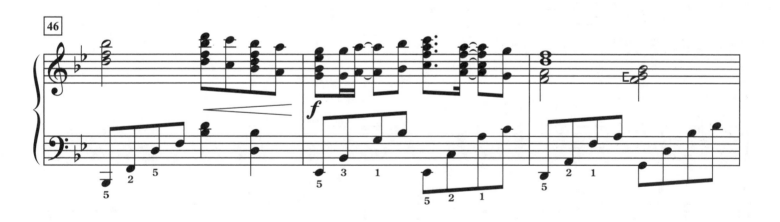

44

(Approx. Performance Time – 2:15)

He Is Exalted

Words and Music by Twila Paris
Arr. Kenon D. Renfrow

Joyfully (♩. = 72)

pedal ad lib.

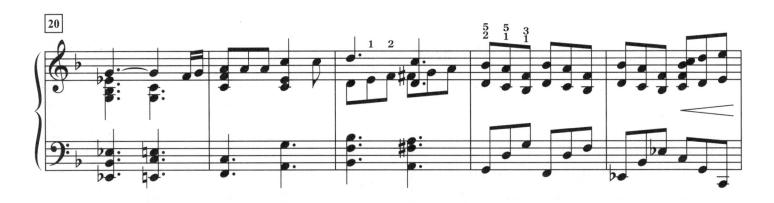

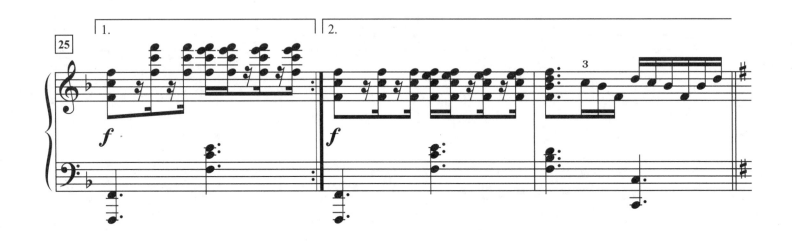

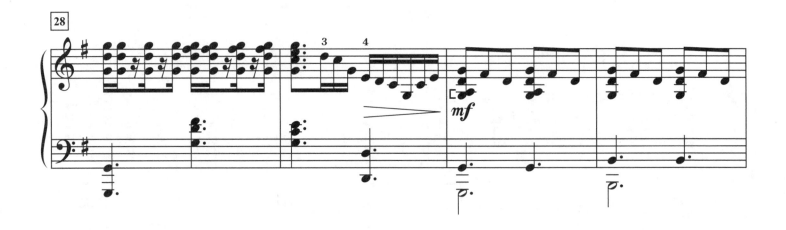